# Soon

Written and
Illustrated
by Jessica Love

ECHO BOOKS

First published in 2015 by Barrallier Books Pty Ltd,
trading as Echo Books.

Registered Office: 35-37 Gordon Avenue, West Geelong, Victoria 3220, Australia.

www.echobooks.com.au

National Library of Australia Cataloguing-in-Publication entry : (paperback)

Creator: Love, Jessica, author, illustrator.

Title: Soon/Jessica Love (author and illustrator).

ISBN: 9780994232397 (paperback)

Target Audience: For primary school age.

Subjects: Soldiers--Family relationships--Australia--Juvenile literature.

Australia--Armed Forces--Juvenile literature.

Dewey Number: 355.10994

Set in Open Dyslexic, Regular 22/30.

Book and cover design by Peter Gamble, Ink Pot Graphic Design, Canberra.

www.echobooks.com.au

*'You just have to put yourself out there in life because believe me anything can happen'*

*Jess Love*

*To Aaron Blabey, for kick starting this amazing adventure!*
*To my parents, without you there wouldn't be a story.*
*To my Mum, for the English assignment!*
*To my brothers, for madness when I need it ...*
*And to children of Defence families, well done for everything, because let's face it, we're pretty amazing.*
*And thank YOU, for reading my book because without you I'd be nowhere.*

My Dad is leaving soon.

He is going to another country to help keep other families safe.

Soon is coming too fast.

My Dad left today.
He says he'll be home soon ...

... but soon is a very long time.

My Dad missed my birthday today.

A card came in the mail. It says he'll be home soon ...

...but soon is so far away.

My Dad rang  today.

He says he is ok and misses me lots.

Talking to him makes me sad ...

... because soon seems like
it will never come.

My Dad sent me a letter today.

Inside are photos of where he has been.

It says he'll be home soon ...

... but soon is still so far away.

My Dad couldn't call today.

We had a big storm.

It scared me.

I wish soon was here.

It is Christmas today.

My Dad is still gone. I am sad.

Christmas feels strange without him ...

... but soon is getting closer.

We moved house today.

When my Dad comes home
I hope he can find us.

Now I know he'll be home soon.

It's my birthday again today.

My Dad is still away ...

... but soon is very close.

My Dad's plane left today.

He rang us before he left.

It is exciting and a little scary.

I wonder if he will be the same ...

... Soon is taking so long.

My Dad came home today.

I am happy but he is very tired.

All he does is sleep.

He is not quite here yet ...

...but soon is a lot, lot closer.

My Dad stopped sleeping today.

He is happy,
so I am happy.

He says he loves me, and ...

... soon is **finally** here.

Dear CDF

Some people think this means Chief of the Defence Force but it stands for someone even more important ...

YOU! ... the Children of Defence Families

Thank you.

Thank you for having the spirit to move house often.

Thank you for being brave enough to attend new schools and make new friends.

Thank you for being so courageous when your Mum or Dad is sent overseas to make our world a better, safer place.

For those of us whose Mum or Dad is away I hope soon comes quickly.

Thank you for putting service before self.

Thank you for YOUR sacrifice.

Jess x

www.ingramcontent.com/pod-product-compliance
Lightning Source LLC
LaVergne TN
LVHW072110070426
835509LV00002B/100

9 780994 232397